A LifeGuide®

LOVE

The Greatest Gift of All

9 studies
for individuals or groups

Phyllis J. Le Peau

With Notes for Leaders

IVP Connect

An imprint of InterVarsity Press
Downers Grove, Illinois

InterVarsity Press
P.O. Box 1400, Downers Grove, IL 60515-1426
World Wide Web: www.ivpress.com
E-mail: email@ivpress.com

InterVarsity Press® is the book-publishing division of InterVarsity Christian Fellowship/USA®, a student movement active on campus at hundreds of universities, colleges and schools of nursing in the United States of America, and a member movement of the International Fellowship of Evangelical Students. For information about local and regional activities, write Public Relations Dept., InterVarsity Christian Fellowship/USA, 6400 Schroeder Rd., P.O. Box 7895, Madison, WI 53707-7895, or visit the IVCF website at <www.intervarsity.org>.

LifeGuide® is a registered trademark of InterVarsity Christian Fellowship.

Some notes in study 6 are adapted from James: Faith That Works, *rev. ed ©1978 by Andrew T. and Phyllis J. Le Peau, and used by permission of InterVarsity Press.*

Cover image: Antony Edwards/Getty Images

ISBN 978-0-8308-3083-1

Printed in the United States of America ∞

P	21	20	19	18	17	16	15	14	13	12	11	10	9	8	7	6
Y	21	20	19	18	17	16	15	14	13	12	11	10	09	08	07	

Contents

Getting the Most Out of *Love*

At the time InterVarsity Press asked for a guide on love, I felt I had never known less about loving others. I could make no claims of loving as Christ calls us to love. I had a critical spirit and, at the very least, sought my own good rather than the good of others. I wasn't even sure I knew how to love my husband and children. I needed to be changed by the Word of God through the work of the Holy Spirit.

As a result of working through the passages in this guide, I have found that I do not know how to love. I cannot love others through my own effort or power. I realized I don't even know how to be loved or to bask in the great love and grace that God pours out on me. I needed (and need constantly) to go back to square one—back to the fundamental life-changing truth that God himself loves me dearly and values me beyond comprehension.

I remember one morning during my quiet time desperately wanting God to change me and my pattern of thinking. I had confessed every sin that came to my memory—every evil attitude that I knew—and still felt no relief. I wondered if I was blocking his work in me, though that was the last thing I wanted to do. Then my mind went back to Romans 8 and the description of God and his everlasting love for me. I turned to that chapter again and read out loud several times that nothing can separate me from God's love—even myself.

From that experience and others, I know that it is only as I know and believe and experience his love that I can even begin to think about loving others. "How great is the love the Father has lavished on us, that we should be called children of God! And that is what we are!" (1 John 3:1). Praise God for his great love for us! God's love for me is the only foundation on which I can build a life of love for others.

I am also reminded through these passages that to love is indeed a choice. A choice that is often difficult and costly. One that may be void of warm, fuzzy feelings. A choice that involves doing the opposite of what my natural inclinations call me to do.

Obeying Christ's command to love others might mean praying for them when I do not feel like praying or when praying takes me away from something that has more obvious benefits. It sometimes means serving others (even when I am treated like a servant). At times, loving others means bending my will in their direction or giving the time and emotional energy that it takes to gently comfort someone in pain.

As you consider God's love for you and what it means to respond to his love by loving others, may you first of all know God and his love deeply and experientially, and from that solid foundation grow in your love for others.

Suggestions for Individual Study

1. As you begin each study, pray that God will speak to you through his Word.

2. Read the introduction to the study and respond to the personal reflection question or exercise. This is designed to help you focus on God and on the theme of the study.

3. Each study deals with a particular passage—so that you can delve into the author's meaning in that context. Read and reread the passage to be studied. The questions are written using the language of the New International Version, so you may wish to use that version of the Bible. The New Revised Standard Version is also recommended.

4. This is an inductive Bible study, designed to help you discover for yourself what Scripture is saying. The study includes three types of questions. *Observation* questions ask about the basic facts: who, what, when, where and how. *Interpretation* questions delve into the meaning of the passage. *Application* questions help you discover the implications of the text for growing in Christ. These three keys unlock the treasures of Scripture.

Write your answers to the questions in the spaces provided or in a personal journal. Writing can bring clarity and deeper understanding of yourself and of God's Word.

5. It might be good to have a Bible dictionary handy. Use it to look up any unfamiliar words, names or places.

6. Use the prayer suggestion to guide you in thanking God for what you have learned and to pray about the applications that have come to mind.

7. You may want to go on to the suggestion under "Now or Later," or you may want to use that idea for your next study.

Suggestions for Members of a Group Study

1. Come to the study prepared. Follow the suggestions for individual study mentioned above. You will find that careful preparation will greatly enrich your time spent in group discussion.

2. Be willing to participate in the discussion. The leader of your group will not be lecturing. Instead, he or she will be encouraging the members of the group to discuss what they have learned. The leader will be asking the questions that are found in this guide.

3. Stick to the topic being discussed. Your answers should be based on the verses which are the focus of the discussion and not on outside authorities such as commentaries or speakers. These studies focus on a particular passage of Scripture. Only rarely should you refer to other portions of the Bible. This allows for everyone to participate in in-depth study on equal ground.

4. Be sensitive to the other members of the group. Listen attentively when they describe what they have learned. You may be surprised by their insights! Each question assumes a variety of answers. Many questions do not have "right" answers, particularly questions that aim at meaning or application. Instead the questions push us to explore the passage more thoroughly.

When possible, link what you say to the comments of others. Also, be affirming whenever you can. This will encourage some of the more hesitant members of the group to participate.

5. Be careful not to dominate the discussion. We are sometimes so eager to express our thoughts that we leave too little opportunity for others to respond. By all means participate! But allow others to also.

6. Expect God to teach you through the passage being discussed and through the other members of the group. Pray that you will have an enjoyable and profitable time together, but also that as a result of the study you will find ways that you can take action individually and/or as a group.

7. Remember that anything said in the group is considered confidential and should not be discussed outside the group unless specific permission is given to do so.

8. If you are the group leader, you will find additional suggestions at the back of the guide.

1

God's Everlasting Love

Romans 8:1-17, 28-39

David Howard, a missionary in Latin America, once met President Figueres of Costa Rica. After that one meeting, whenever their paths crossed, the president would greet David by name. It was a thrill for David to have someone of such stature recognize him personally!

Have you ever stopped to think about God's stature when he says, "I know you. I love you"? It is one thing to be on a first-name basis with the president of a country. But the God of the universe? Yet it is in fact this God of creation who says, "I know you. And more than know you, I love you so much I will do all I can to meet your deepest needs."

GROUP DISCUSSION. How do you know when someone really loves you?

PERSONAL REFLECTION. How are you affected when you are deeply loved by someone?

In this study we will consider what it is to be secure in God's everlasting love. *Read Romans 8:1-17.*

1. How does Paul describe our condition when we lived by the sinful nature (vv. 5-8)?

2. What all did God do for us even while we were in this awful condition (vv. 1-4, 9-11, 13-17)?

3. What does it mean to you that you can call God *Abba,* a term meaning "dearest Father" (v. 15)?

4. How have you experienced the freedom from condemnation that God's love brings?

How is this freedom different from or similar to what you have experienced of human love?

5. *Read Romans 8:28-39.* According to these verses, what does God do for those who are led by the Spirit of God?

6. Look at Paul's explanation in verses 28-30. Why can he say with such conviction that in all things God works for our good?

How have you recently seen this to be true?

7. In your own words, how does Paul describe and respond to this love of God (vv. 31-39)?

8. Why is being loved like this life-changing?

9. What fears or concerns do you have about your future?

What encouragement about the future can you find in this text?

---

10. How do you respond to the evidence in this passage of God's great love for you?

Use words from this passage to describe the love of God and praise him for it. Talk to him about the difficulty you have believing and experiencing his love. Ask him to make very real to you the fact that "nothing can separate you from God's love."

Now or Later

Go back through the passage and list what God has done for you, is doing for you and will do for you. Note God's attitude toward you in all that he is doing. Write out a letter of praise to God. In it tell him where you have trouble believing and accepting his love. Ask him to open your heart and mind to believe it and be transformed by it.

2

God's Unlimited Love

Romans 4:18—5:11

My friend and his father traveled together across the country from California to Boston. They took time to savor the majesty of what they saw. They bought a simple box camera in order to preserve the beauty that they observed and to share their experience with the rest of the family. The first thing they did when they arrived in Boston was to get the film developed. The family gathered around the dining room table, eager to view the pictures. When they pulled out the pictures from the first envelope, they found no beautiful trees or flowers or magnificent mountains. Instead they saw an ugly building or an unknown person or a blank space. On the right side of each picture was a human ear. They had looked through the wrong side of the camera! What a disappointment. They had focused on the wrong image.

GROUP DISCUSSION. What helps you to focus on God and his love?

PERSONAL REFLECTION. Write out a paragraph that begins, "When I focus on God and his love I . . ."

In this study we will see what a difference it makes when we focus on the right image, God and his great, unlimited love! *Read Romans 4:18-25.*

1. How did Abraham respond to God's promise that he would be the forebearer of millions of people?

2. Note key facts about Abraham in verse 19. If you were in his situation, would you find it hard to trust God? Why or why not?

3. How were Abraham's faith and life affected by the fact that he focused on God?

4. How does Abraham's situation connect with ours (vv. 23-25)?

5. *Read Romans 5:1-11.* We, like Abraham, are justified through faith. What are the fruits of this justification as seen throughout this passage?

6. Paul states that by faith, we not only have access into God's grace, but we also stand in that grace (5:2). Compare and contrast what it means to have access into grace with what it means to stand in that grace.

7. Paul names two sources of rejoicing (5:1-5). Explain each and how they are similar and different.

8. What is the connection between hope and the glory of God (5:2-5)?

9. When have you experienced hope because suffering resulted in a change of character in yourself or in others?

10. According to 5:6-10, how does God demonstrate his love for us?

11. What difference do the acts of God's love described in this passage make in your everyday life?

12. What in this passage helps you most to focus on God and his great love for you?

Tell God how you feel about the fact that he has justified you through the death of his Son. Ask his Spirit to reveal to you how God has poured out his love into your life. Ask God to help you to focus on him and his love.

Now or Later

Journal about where you are suffering. Write a brief description of the situation in the first paragraph. In the second jot down where you see God in the midst of this suffering, if you do. In the third paragraph jot down how you need to see God and how you might focus on him more. Continue the journal for as many days as it takes you to complete. Make it a guide for conversations with the Lord throughout the week.

3

Responding to God's Love

When our children were small, "I love you, Mom" and "I love you Dad" came out of their mouths with such ease. We were thrilled every time we heard them. As they reached the teen years, their expressions of affection were less frequent. That made their affirming words more meaningful than ever. God, our heavenly Father, enjoys our expressions of love for him every bit as much as, and more than, earthly parents do.

GROUP DISCUSSION. Think of someone that you love dearly. What are some ways that you show your love to that person?

PERSONAL REFLECTION. How do you usually respond to the words "I love you"?

In this study we will consider how we respond to God's love by obeying him. *Read John 15:1-8.*

1. What initial thoughts, feelings or questions do you have about this text?

2. In the analogy of the vineyard describe what represents the Father, Jesus and the disciples?

3. Why is it vital for branches to remain in the vine?

4. According to this passage, what does it mean to remain in Jesus (vv. 2-3, 5-7)?

How does this happen?

5. When have you experienced pruning?

6. What role do the Word of God and prayer play in your bearing of fruit?

7. *Read John 15:9-17.* According to verses 9-10, what added dimensions does remaining in Christ take on?

8. What are the results of obeying Jesus' commands?

9. Verse 12 tells us to love each other as Jesus loves us. How has Jesus loved us?

10. As you consider how Jesus has loved you, how does that affect your obeying his command to love others?

11. In verses 13-16 Jesus calls us his friends. How does what you learn about being Jesus' friend enrich your understanding of your connection to him?

12. Jesus promises that as we abide in him, the Father will give us what we ask for. What prayers have you seen answered recently?

13. In this passage Jesus has told us how to be fruitful and that the fruit we bear will last (v. 16). How does this help us understand what our priorities should be?

Praise Jesus who is the true vine and the Father who is the gardener. Talk to the Lord about areas in your life where you long to see fruit.

Now or Later

Reflect on the three categories of branches described in this passage— those bearing no fruit, those bearing some fruit and those bearing much fruit. Generally, in which category would you place yourself? Why?

Now think through specific areas of your life, such as the time you spend with God, sharing the gospel and serving others. How would you evaluate your fruit bearing? In what areas of your life do you long to bear fruit?

4

Love That Serves

2 Kings 4:8-37

Fat cells are servants to the rest of the body. By themselves they are useless and can even become hazardous when there are too many of them. But there is great value to fat. Every fat cell is a storehouse of oil. When famine comes to the body due to lack of other sources of energy, the signal of need is sent out by the brain. The fat cells then release oil that is fuel for the needed energy. This energy is essential for the other cells of the body to do their jobs. So in a sense fat cells exist purely to serve the rest of the body.

In a real sense, like fat cells, we exist to serve God and each other. Love is the core of serving in this way.

GROUP DISCUSSION. How have others served you over this past week?

PERSONAL REFLECTION. How do you feel after serving someone else?

In this study we see how love is demonstrated by serving others. *Read 2 Kings 4:8-16.*

1. Describe the ways the Shunammite woman served Elisha and her motivations for doing so.

2. What motivates you to serve others?

3. What inhibits you from serving others?

4. What does Elisha's request in verse 13 reveal about him?

5. Though the woman stated no needs, Elisha offered her a son. Why do you think she responded in the way she did (v. 16)?

6. How willing are you to make your needs known and to allow someone to serve you? Explain.

When have you felt suspicious when someone served you?

---

7. *Read 2 Kings 4:17-37.* In your own words tell what happened to this woman.

---

8. What evidence is there throughout these verses that she believed that Elisha would help her?

---

9. How do you see Elisha going beyond the call of duty to serve her?

---

10. How does this story illustrate the great value of serving one another?

---

11. How might you express God's love to others this week by serving them?

Thank Jesus that he, Lord of the universe, came to serve. Ask God to free you to be able to make your needs known to others as well as make you sensitive to the needs of others.

Now or Later

The Shunammite woman served Elisha through hospitality. In our culture opening our homes to people is becoming rare. How do you feel about loving others by opening your home to them? What are specific ways that you can do this? Look at your calendar and think about ways to plan events in which you will intentionally serve and love others through hospitality.

5

Love That Submits

1 Samuel 3

"If anyone had any questions about our building campaign consultant, they should have been answered tonight," the moderator of the elders' board told my husband, Andy.

"Well, I'll find out on my way home," he replied cautiously.

It was time to build a church. The elders had decided to hire a consultant. I not only felt this was a bad idea, I felt it strongly. It seemed to me that a consultant was not the best use of our money. I thought it would be best if our own leaders could prayerfully guide us through this process.

Andy, on the other hand, was not only totally in favor of hiring a consultant, he had taken the lead in persuading the congregation! I could not get him to change his mind. All my finest logic and persuasive words made absolutely no impact on him. He had continued to vigorously type up his "propaganda" for the congregation even as I talked.

I had a choice to make. I could continue to battle them all, or I could bend my will toward that of my husband and the leaders of our church. What would be the godly choice at this point—to fight for my convictions or to submit to the wisdom of others?

GROUP DISCUSSION. Why is it sometimes difficult to submit to someone else?

PERSONAL REFLECTION. Think about a time when you had a particularly difficult time submitting your will to that of another. What did it feel like? What helped you to get through it?

This passage helps us to understand the unnatural but sometimes necessary route of submission. *Read 1 Samuel 3.*

---

1. What basic facts do you learn about the two main characters in this story, Samuel and Eli?

---

2. Throughout this passage, what evidence of an attitude of submission do you see in Samuel?

---

3. How does your attitude of submission compare or contrast to that of Samuel?

---

4. How did his relationship and submission to Eli affect his relationship with God?

5. How have you found that your relationship with God is affected by your willingness or lack of willingness to submit to others?

6. Why is submitting to others evidence of loving them?

7. Submission does not mean mindlessly doing what someone else says. When might it be wrong to submit to another?

8. What did Samuel hear from God (vv. 11-14)?

9. When have you experienced the Lord speaking to you through another person or to another person through you?

10. How do you listen to God?

What hinders you from listening to him?

---

11. What were the long-term results of submission in Samuel's life (vv. 19-21)?

---

12. How do you need to grow in the area of submitting to others?

to God?

Talk to God about your difficulty in bending your will to submit to godly leaders. Confess ways in which you fail to submit to God as well. Ask God to forgive you and make your heart soft and open to loving others by submitting to them.

Now or Later

In some circles, submission is known as the "'S' word." But in the Scriptures we see it as a positive action toward others. Jesus submitted to the will of God and went to the cross. Paul calls us to "submit to one another out of reverence for Christ" in Ephesians 5. Submission is always voluntarily given, never forced by someone else. List areas where you have difficulty "bending your will toward another." Take the list to a pastor, counselor or trusted friend. Talk and pray through the list with them.

6

Love That Prays

James 5:13-20

Just yesterday I was a parent of small children, infants and toddlers. Today, I am the parent of adolescents and young adults. Yesterday, with just a word or a hug—or for sure an M&M—I had great influence on my children. Today I seem to have very little. Or at best, the less I say the greater the influence. Unless, of course, I am talking about them to our heavenly Father. So when a friend of ours said, "I am praying for your children daily," I gratefully replied, "There is no better way to love us or them."

GROUP DISCUSSION. How do you feel when you know someone is praying for you regularly?

PERSONAL REFLECTION. Who would you like to pray for faithfully? How would you like to pray for them?

In this passage we will consider loving others by praying for them. *Read James 5:13-20.*

1. In your own words describe all the situations in which prayer is recommended.

2. What is your usual first response when you are in trouble?

3. Why do you think we are encouraged to call the elders of the church to pray for and anoint us when we are sick (v. 14)?

4. Describe a time when you have prayed for physical healing for others or when others have prayed for it for you.

5. How is praying for others when they are sick or in trouble the same as loving them?

6. According to verses 15 and 16, what does God promise us when we pray for each other?

---

7. Verse 16 tells us to confess our sins to each other. What hinders you from confessing your sins to others?

---

8. When have you experienced the healing effect (physical, emotional, spiritual or psychological) of confessing your sins to others?

---

9. The story of Elijah demonstrates what can be accomplished by someone's prayer. How do you respond to the promise that "the prayer of a righteous person is powerful and effective"?

---

10. Verse 19 suggests a vital way of loving brothers and sisters. What does it mean for someone to "wander from the truth"?

11. What role do you think prayer plays in bringing back a wandering brother or sister?

---

12. How would you like to grow in living a life of love that prays?

Ask God to reveal to you those for whom you should pray regularly. Ask him to give you people who will pray for you. Thank him for those who have demonstrated their love to you by praying for you.

Now or Later

Consider practical ways of growing your prayer life. Some possibilities are to make a prayer list and record answers to prayer; invite someone to be a prayer partner and pray together regularly; plan a regular time and place to pray daily; pray through a passage of Scripture regularly. Choose at least one to implement into your life.

7

Love That Comforts

2 Corinthians 1:1-11

We are tempted to think how wonderful life would be if there were no pain. However, Paul Brand and Philip Yancey point out in their book *Fearfully and Wonderfully Made* how important pain is, as are the nerve cells that transmit pain. If our skin is damaged and these nerve endings are not functioning, we are in grave danger of destroying the rest of our body. We do not have the warning of danger that pain provides for us.

Pain also plays a definite role in the body of Christ and in our lives. For the sake of the church I need to be in tune with pain, my own as well as that of others. We need to heed its warning and allow pain to do its work.

GROUP DISCUSSION. What helps when you feel loss, sadness or hurt?

PERSONAL REFLECTION. What comfort do you need from God today? Sit and wait for him to visit you with peace and reassurance.

In the midst of our suffering we are able to receive God's comfort and as a result, love others by comforting them. *Read 2 Corinthians 1:1-11.*

1. How does Paul's greeting in verses 1-2 set the tone for what follows?

2. How do you respond to the description of our heavenly Father in this passage (vv. 3-7)?

3. What is the connection between Christ's suffering and his comfort (vv. 5-6)?

4. Paul speaks about God's comfort from his own personal experience. Describe the suffering that he and his colleagues experienced (vv. 8-9).

5. What did God do for them (v. 10)?

6. When have you experienced God's comfort in a difficult situation?

7. How did your experience of God's comfort help you to comfort others?

8. In verses 8-11 what did Paul learn about suffering?

9. Based on God's faithfulness to them, they set their hope on him. How does this affect your sense of hope in God when in the midst of suffering?

10. How did the Corinthians help Paul (v. 11)?

11. In summary, what is Paul's attitude toward his suffering through-out this passage?

12. How does this mutuality of love between Paul and the Corin-thians show that we are strengthened in Christ even as we seek to help others?

Praise God that suffering is not meaningless in the life of a Christian. Talk to God about Paul's attitude toward his suffering; ask God to make your attitude like Paul's.

Now or Later

Ask God to lead you to one or two people who are suffering and give you the opportunity to comfort and minister to them.

8

Love That Forgives

Matthew 18:21-35

When Andy and I considered God's call to marriage, we were surrounded by love and wisdom from those in our Christian community. One particular bit of counsel that continues to affect the vitality of our relationship is, "Do not ever withhold forgiveness from one another." This urgency to forgive is not only important in the marriage relationship; it is essential to every human relationship.

GROUP DISCUSSION. How are you affected when you carry a grudge against someone?

PERSONAL REFLECTION. Who have you not forgiven? Why?

In this passage Jesus demands that Christians forgive one another and that there be no limit to this love that forgives. *Read Matthew 18:21-35.*

1. Behind Peter's question in verse 21 was the Jewish teaching that to forgive someone three times was reasonable. Knowing this, how would you describe the exchange between Peter and Jesus in verses 21-22?

2. What do you think keeps Christians from forgiving each other?

3. Not content to let the matter rest with forgiving seventy-seven times, Jesus proceeded to elaborate his statement with a parable. Why did the king in the parable originally forgive the servant's debt (v. 27)?

4. How did the king go far beyond what the servant requested (vv. 26-27)?

5. What is your reaction to the servant's actions toward his fellow servant in verses 28-30? Why?

6. How did the first servant's debt compare with that of the second servant?

7. In this parable who do each of the characters represent?

What do each of the debts represent?

8. How do your wrongs against God compare with the ways others have wronged you?

9. How do you reconcile Jesus' advocating unlimited forgiveness while in the parable, the king retracts his forgiveness of the servant who didn't forgive his fellow servant (vv. 32-35)?

10. What does it mean to forgive one another "from the heart"?

11. In this passage how does Jesus demonstrate God's seriousness about forgiving one another?

12. How do you need to grow in loving others by forgiving them?

Ask God to give you a heart overflowing with forgiveness for others. Ask him to bring to your mind those you need to forgive and those you need to ask for forgiveness.

Now or Later

Think of someone that you need to forgive and someone from whom you need forgiveness. Ask God to lead you in the steps you need to take in beginning reconciliation.

9

Love That Unites

World War I, the massive conflict at the beginning of the twentieth century that resulted in the deaths of over ten million soldiers, began with the death of a single individual. On July 28, 1914, Archduke Franz Ferdinand, the heir to the Austrian throne, was shot while riding in a motorcar through Sarajevo. This incident triggered the network of alliances that were in place among the European nations, and war raged for the next four years.

Huge conflict can also break out in our homes and Christian communities because of small incidents that get blown out of proportion. We are called as Christians to love one another. This love is lived out in the small practicalities of life. The outcome of loving this way is a life of peace and unity.

GROUP DISCUSSION. How are you affected when you hear music with beautiful harmony?

PERSONAL REFLECTION. While you listen to a piece of beautiful music, think about God and praise him for creating this marvelous harmony.

In this study we will consider practical ways of loving God and each other. *Read Romans 12:1-8.*

1. What aspects of God's character are the foundation for all that Paul calls us to in this passage (vv. 1, 3, 6)?

2. How are the body, mind and spirit shown to be vitally linked in spiritual worship?

How does this relate to your experience of worship?

3. According to verses 3-8, how is harmony found within the body of Christ?

4. Which of the guidelines is most challenging to you? Why?

5. *Read Romans 12:9-21.* These verses continue to give practical direction for living out God's good, pleasing and perfect will. List the instructions that are given.

6. What do you think it means to "honor one another above yourselves" (v. 10)?

What helps you to do this?

7. How would being "joyful in hope, patient in affliction, faithful in prayer" affect your relationship with others (v. 12)?

8. How can you practice hospitality and share with others who are in need (v. 13)?

9. How are the instructions in verses 14-21 particularly helpful in living at peace with everyone?

10. How would being "devoted to one another in brotherly love" support and undergird all that we are called to be in this chapter (v. 10)?

11. As you look back over the instructions given in this passage, in what areas do you need to grow the most?

Ask God to make your love more like his so that those around you will know him better.

Now or Later

Go back over this chapter. List the guidelines given for living a life of peace and unity. Now think of one step that you will take for each guideline. Write those steps down and begin implementing them.

Leader's Notes

MY GRACE IS SUFFICIENT FOR YOU. (2 COR 12:9)

Leading a Bible discussion can be an enjoyable and rewarding experience. But it can also be *scary*—especially if you've never done it before. If this is your feeling, you're in good company. When God asked Moses to lead the Israelites out of Egypt, he replied, "O Lord, please send someone else to do it"! (Ex 4:13). It was the same with Solomon, Jeremiah and Timothy, but God helped these people in spite of their weaknesses, and he will help you as well.

You don't need to be an expert on the Bible or a trained teacher to lead a Bible discussion. The idea behind these inductive studies is that the leader guides group members to discover for themselves what the Bible has to say. This method of learning will allow group members to remember much more of what is said than a lecture would.

These studies are designed to be led easily. As a matter of fact, the flow of questions through the passage from observation to interpretation to application is so natural that you may feel that the studies lead themselves. This study guide is also flexible. You can use it with a variety of groups—student, professional, neighborhood or church groups. Each study takes forty-five to sixty minutes in a group setting.

There are some important facts to know about group dynamics and encouraging discussion. The suggestions listed below should enable you to effectively and enjoyably fulfill your role as leader.

Preparing for the Study

1. Ask God to help you understand and apply the passage in your own life. Unless this happens, you will not be prepared to lead others. Pray too for the various members of the group. Ask God to open your hearts to the message of his Word and motivate you to action.

2. Read the introduction to the entire guide to get an overview of the entire book and the issues which will be explored.

3. As you begin each study, read and reread the assigned Bible passage to familiarize yourself with it.

4. This study guide is based on the New International Version of the Bible. It will help you and the group if you use this translation as the basis for your study and discussion.

5. Carefully work through each question in the study. Spend time in meditation and reflection as you consider how to respond.

6. Write your thoughts and responses in the space provided in the study guide. This will help you to express your understanding of the passage clearly.

7. It might help to have a Bible dictionary handy. Use it to look up any unfamiliar words, names or places. (For additional help on how to study a passage, see chapter five of *How to Lead a LifeGuide® Bible Study,* InterVarsity Press.)

8. Consider how you can apply the Scripture to your life. Remember that the group will follow your lead in responding to the studies. They will not go any deeper than you do.

9. Once you have finished your own study of the passage, familiarize yourself with the leader's notes for the study you are leading. These are designed to help you in several ways. First, they tell you the purpose the study guide author had in mind when writing the study. Take time to think through how the study questions work together to accomplish that purpose. Second, the notes provide you with additional background information or suggestions on group dynamics for various questions. This information can be useful when people have difficulty understanding or answering a question. Third, the leader's notes can alert you to potential problems you may encounter during the study.

10. If you wish to remind yourself of anything mentioned in the leader's notes, make a note to yourself below that question in the study.

Leading the Study

1. Begin the study on time. Open with prayer, asking God to help the group to understand and apply the passage.

2. Be sure that everyone in your group has a study guide. Encourage the group to prepare beforehand for each discussion by reading the introduction to the guide and by working through the questions in the study.

3. At the beginning of your first time together, explain that these studies are meant to be discussions, not lectures. Encourage the members of the group to participate. However, do not put pressure on those who may be hesitant to speak during the first few sessions. You may want to suggest the following guidelines to your group.

☐ Stick to the topic being discussed.

☐ Your responses should be based on the verses which are the focus of the discussion and not on outside authorities such as commentaries or speakers.

☐ These studies focus on a particular passage of Scripture. Only rarely should you refer to other portions of the Bible. This allows for everyone to participate in in-depth study on equal ground.

☐ Anything said in the group is considered confidential and will not be discussed outside the group unless specific permission is given to do so.

☐ We will listen attentively to each other and provide time for each person present to talk.

☐ We will pray for each other.

4. Have a group member read the introduction at the beginning of the discussion.

5. Every session begins with a group discussion question. The question or activity is meant to be used before the passage is read. The question introduces the theme of the study and encourages group members to begin to open up. Encourage as many members as possible to participate, and be ready to get the discussion going with your own response.

This section is designed to reveal where our thoughts or feelings need to be transformed by Scripture. That is why it is especially important not to read the passage before the discussion question is asked. The passage will tend to color the honest reactions people would otherwise give because they are, of course, supposed to think the way the Bible does.

You may want to supplement the group discussion question with an icebreaker to help people to get comfortable. See the community section of *Small Group Idea Book* for more ideas.

You also might want to use the personal reflection question with your group. Either allow a time of silence for people to respond individually or discuss it together.

6. Have a group member (or members if the passage is long) read aloud the passage to be studied. Then give people several minutes to read the passage again silently so that they can take it all in.

7. Question 1 will generally be an overview question designed to briefly survey the passage. Encourage the group to look at the whole passage, but try to avoid getting sidetracked by questions or issues that will be addressed later in the study.

8. As you ask the questions, keep in mind that they are designed to be used just as they are written. You may simply read them aloud. Or you may prefer to express them in your own words.

There may be times when it is appropriate to deviate from the study guide.

For example, a question may have already been answered. If so, move on to the next question. Or someone may raise an important question not covered in the guide. Take time to discuss it, but try to keep the group from going off on tangents.

9. Avoid answering your own questions. If necessary, repeat or rephrase them until they are clearly understood. Or point out something you read in the leader's notes to clarify the context or meaning. An eager group quickly becomes passive and silent if they think the leader will do most of the talking.

10. Don't be afraid of silence. People may need time to think about the question before formulating their answers.

11. Don't be content with just one answer. Ask, "What do the rest of you think?" or "Anything else?" until several people have given answers to the question.

12. Acknowledge all contributions. Try to be affirming whenever possible. Never reject an answer. If it is clearly off-base, ask, "Which verse led you to that conclusion?" or again, "What do the rest of you think?"

13. Don't expect every answer to be addressed to you, even though this will probably happen at first. As group members become more at ease, they will begin to truly interact with each other. This is one sign of healthy discussion.

14. Don't be afraid of controversy. It can be very stimulating. If you don't resolve an issue completely, don't be frustrated. Move on and keep it in mind for later. A subsequent study may solve the problem.

15. Periodically summarize what the group has said about the passage. This helps to draw together the various ideas mentioned and gives continuity to the study. But don't preach.

16. At the end of the Bible discussion you may want to allow group members a time of quiet to work on an idea under "Now or Later." Then discuss what you experienced. Or you may want to encourage group members to work on these ideas between meetings. Give an opportunity during the session for people to talk about what they are learning.

17. Conclude your time together with conversational prayer, adapting the prayer suggestion at the end of the study to your group. Ask for God's help in following through on the commitments you've made.

18. End on time.

Many more suggestions and helps are found in *How to Lead a LifeGuide®️ Bible Study.*

Components of Small Groups

A healthy small group should do more than study the Bible. There are four components to consider as you structure your time together.

Nurture. Small groups help us to grow in our knowledge and love of God. Bible study is the key to making this happen and is the foundation of your small group.

Community. Small groups are a great place to develop deep friendships with other Christians. Allow time for informal interaction before and after each study. Plan activities and games that will help you get to know each other. Spend time having fun together—going on a picnic or cooking dinner together.

Worship and prayer. Your study will be enhanced by spending time praising God together in prayer or song. Pray for each other's needs—and keep track of how God is answering prayer in your group. Ask God to help you to apply what you are learning in your study.

Outreach. Reaching out to others can be a practical way of applying what you are learning, and it will keep your group from becoming self-focused. Host a series of evangelistic discussions for your friends or neighbors. Clean up the yard of an elderly friend. Serve at a soup kitchen together, or spend a day working on a Habitat house.

Many more suggestions and helps in each of these areas are found in *Small Group Idea Book.* Information on building a small group can be found in *Small Group Leaders' Handbook* and *The Big Book on Small Groups* (both from Inter-Varsity Press). Reading through one of these books would be worth your time.

Study 1. God's Everlasting Love. Romans 8:1-17, 28-39.

Purpose: To understand and experience our value to God, his love for us and the fact that nothing can separate us from him or his love.

General note. Ask God to make the truth of this passage and his love real to you as you prepare and lead the group. Pray for yourself and each member of your group that you will grow in the knowledge and experience of God's love.

Group discussion. Every study begins with a "group discussion" question, which is meant to be asked before the passage is read. These questions are important for several reasons.

First, they help the group to warm up to each other. No matter how well a group may know each other, there is always a stiffness that needs to be overcome before people will begin to talk openly. A good question will break the ice.

Second, the questions get people thinking along the lines of the topic of the study. Most people will have lots of different things going on in their mind (dinner, an important meeting coming up, how to get the car fixed) that will have nothing to do with the study. A creative question will get their attention and draw them into the discussion.

Third, the questions can reveal where our thoughts or feelings need to be transformed by Scripture. That is why it is especially important not to read the passage before the questions are asked.

Personal reflection. These questions are designed for individuals studying on their own. If you wish, you could allow group members to silently reflect on the question. Then you could ask a general question about what they experienced in their time of personal reflection (rather than having them answer the question aloud). Or you could simply move on to the Scripture reading.

Questions 1-2. Take the time to look at this information carefully. You will need to direct the group through all seventeen verses to get a complete view of our condition when we lived by the sinful nature as well as all that God did for us while we were in this awful condition. Be prepared to lead the discussion so that serious consideration will be given to this condition. In other words, you don't want your group just to list facts. Feel free to add questions for depth or clarification as you go along. In order to appreciate what God did for us, we need to realize our state of need—mentally *and* emotionally.

Question 3. For those who have a loving earthly father, the response to this question could be significantly different than for those who have experienced an absent or abusive father. The latter group might have difficulty accepting the role of God as their daddy as a positive thing because they have not known the love of a faithful earthly father. Some could be in the midst of healing from an abusive or absent father as a result of knowing the love and presence of a heavenly Father. This process could begin even with this study. Allow free expression of emotion and questions.

Question 5. In the previous verses we have considered what God did for us in our past (when we lived by the sinful nature) and what he has planned for our future. In this portion, we are looking at what he is doing for us right now (though, of course, what he has done in our past and for our future affects us right now too).

Question 6. These verses give us hope because they explain "the good" that he works for. This good is that we be conformed to the likeness of Jesus. It does not mean that all things will make us feel happy or successful as the world measures prosperity. But the "all things" in our lives will move us toward conformity to Jesus and glorification.

Use the second part of the question to make it concrete. Don't allow group members to go on too long with this however. More application questions will come later in the study.

Questions 7-8. Do what you can to help the group to feel the power of Paul's response to the love of God. It is much too easy for us to just repeat facts and descriptions from Scripture without getting into the implications for us. Paul is excited in his response to God. Add your own questions to enhance discussion and perception of God's great love. Pick out phrases such as, "If God is for us, who can be against us?" and "He who did not spare his own son, but gave him up for us all—how will he not also . . . graciously give us all things?" If time allows, you might ask, "What actions would be comparable to giving up your own child?

Question 9. Consider what you have learned about what it means to be a child of God, your future in heaven and your life now. How might that give confidence that God will provide for you now?

Question 10. It is important to attempt to provide an environment for an honest response. This is purposely worded "how do you respond" not "how should you respond." Throughout this guide, the goal is to know and experience God's great love. For some this will begin if they are able to say, "I do not or cannot respond," or "I don't believe it." We can trust the Holy Spirit to reveal God's love to those who are open and honest before him.

Prayer. Each study ends with a simple suggestion regarding themes for prayer that can be used to wrap up the group time.

Study 2. God's Unlimited Love. Romans 4:18—5:11.

Purpose: To experience the difference that God's love makes in our daily life.

Question 4. There are at least two ways that Abraham's situation compares to ours. The first is that we are saved: "God will credit righteousness—for us who believe," just as righteousness was credited to Abraham who believed God. Second, there are situations in daily life in which we need to believe God "against all hope"—believe that he has the power to do what he says he will do even when it looks impossible. For instance, I must believe God has the power to save me and make me as if I had never sinned when it feels like the opposite is true because the evil in me is so great. John Bunyan wrote it this way:

> As I was walking up and down in the house, as a man in a most woeful state, that word of God took hold of my heart, Ye are "justified freely by his grace, through the redemption that is in Christ Jesus" (Romans 3:24). But oh, what a turn it made upon me! Now I was one awakened out of some troublesome sleep and dream, and listening to this heavenly sentence, I was as if I had heard it thus expounded to me:
>
> Sinner, thou thinkest that because of thy sins and infirmities I cannot save thy soul, but behold my Son is by me, and upon him I look,

and not on thee, and will deal with thee according as I am pleased with him. (John Bunyan, *Grace Abounding*, pp. 257-58)

The *New Bible Commentary* highlights John Calvin's application of this paragraph: "Let us also remember, that the condition of us all is the same with that of Abraham. All things around us are in opposition to the promises of God: He promises immortality; we are surrounded with mortality and corruption: He declares that he counts us as just; we are covered with sins" (G. J. Wenham, J. A. Motyer, D. A. Carson and R. T. France, eds., 21st Century Edition [Downers Grove, Ill.: InterVarsity Press, 1994], p. 1132).

Like Abraham I have to look at the facts in my life that make it seem impossible for God to do what he promised and still know that he has the power to keep his promise. If I see a friend turning away from the Lord and making decisions that could ruin her life, I must believe that God has the power to complete the work that he has begun in her as he promised in Philippians 1:6.

Question 5. This is an overview question to help the group move through these verses. John Stott notes six fruits (peace with God, access to and standing in God's grace, rejoicing in our hope of the glory of God, rejoicing in our sufferings, being saved through Christ and rejoicing in God) from being justified by faith in this list. However, the specific number of fruits doesn't matter. In working through the passage, group members might name such things as suffering produces patience or that change in character produces hope. These are all aspects of the benefits that we receive. It is important to see (not just with our physical eyes but with our hearts) all the benefits that are ours when we are justified.

Question 6. Not only do we get to enter into a relationship with God (access into grace) we can enjoy a permanent lasting relationship (in which we stand). We stand in grace; we do not fall in and out of grace. We need God's unmerited favor both to have a relationship with him and to enjoy that relationship forever. We need grace to be saved, and we need God's grace to live in faith. As Christians, we are very aware of his grace which saves, but often less aware of our need for his grace that keeps us and is vital to live out our faith.

Question 8. Here's what John Stott has to say:

Christian hope is not uncertain like our ordinary everyday hopes about the weather or our health; it is a joyful and confident expectation which rests on the promises of God, as we saw in the case of Abraham. And the object of our hope is *the glory of God*, namely his radiant being continuously revealed in the heavens and the earth. Already it has been uniquely made manifest in Jesus Christ, the incarnate Word, most notably in his death and resurrection. One day, however, the curtain will be raised and the glory of God will be fully disclosed. First, Jesus Christ himself will appear "with the great power and glory." Secondly, we will not only see his glory, but be changed into it, so that he will "be glorified in his holy people." Then redeemed human beings, who were created to be "the image and glory of God," but now through sin "fall short of the glory of God" (3:23), will again and in full measure share in his glory (8:17). Thirdly, even the groaning creation "will be liberated from its bondage to decay and brought into the glorious freedom of the children of God" (8:21). The renewed universe will be suffused with its Creator's glory. (*Romans* [Downers Grove, Ill.: InterVarsity Press, 1994], pp. 140-41.)

Question 9. This question can lead into a deeper level of discussion. Think it through for yourself and be ready to talk about changes in your own character that did or could have resulted from the suffering that you have experienced. Sometimes my greatest discouragement is what I perceive as lack of change in me. Therefore, it is a great source of hope when I am able to see God working in my character or in others, and this often happens as a result of suffering.

It is important to provide an environment for honest sharing and "family talk." Some in your group may be angry at God because of suffering in their own lives or the lives of others.

Question 10. Note that verses 9-10 emphasize the sanctification process that happens in our life after we become Christians. We are not only saved, we are *being* saved—changed, made into Christ's image.

Question 11. Unless we are experiencing the truth of God in our lives, looking at Scripture can become a purely academic process.

Study 3. Responding to God's Love. John 15:1-17.
Purpose: To understand Jesus' teaching that God loves us, and to continue in that love and respond to it by obeying him and loving others.

Questions 4-6. You will need to help the group to look closely to see what the passage says in question 3 and then to apply the content to questions 4 and 5.

To remain in Jesus means to stay close enough to him to be nourished by him. It means being connected to our source of life and vitality. It means to draw all our strength from him. This happens through pruning, through the Word, by not trying to produce fruit on our own and through prayer.

If there is time you might want to add the question, "How do you need to be pruned?" to question 5. "How does the Word cleanse you?" and "How does prayer help you to remain in Jesus?" can be used as follow-up questions for question 6.

Question 7. Remaining in Christ takes on the added dimension of "remaining in his love." This is accomplished through obedience to Jesus even as he remains in the Father's love by obeying his Father.

Questions 9-10. Lead the group in discussing the many ways that Jesus has loved us. He has laid down his life for us, served us, made us his friends, made us fruitful and so on. When we think about how Jesus loves us, we realize how our love pales in comparison and how unnatural it is for us to love others in the way that Jesus loves. Help the group to discuss how they struggle with loving others.

Question 13. You might first help the group to savor the fact that the fruit we bear lasts forever. If you have time, ask them how they respond to that fact. Then move into the understanding of priorities based on that fact.

Study 4. Love That Serves. 2 Kings 4:8-37.

Purpose: To observe an example of love that is demonstrated by serving one another and the benefits of this service.

Question 1. She seemed to be motivated by the fact that Elisha was a holy man of God. He was doing God's service, which involved travel, and she wanted to provide a place for him. She wanted to make his life easier and enjoyable. Based on verse 13 it seems clear that her motivation was not to get something for herself. She did not expect or need Elisha to do anything for her.

Question 4. He wanted to serve her. Service from a heart of love will bring a similar response. He was grateful, and being grateful is a state of humility, acknowledging that others are able to give to us and help us.

Question 5. According to the *New Bible Commentary,* "The promise of a son in improbable circumstances is similar to the promise God made to Abraham and Sarah (Gn 18:10), and the woman's sceptical response recalls Sarah's on that occasion (Gn 18:12). But the prophet's word proved trustworthy" (p. 366).

Question 6. As we all well know, often it is much easier to serve others than to allow our own needs to be known and to receive from others. This can be the sin of pride and should be dealt with in a loving Christian community. Be ready for an assortment of answers. Provide an environment that is safe and where responses are accepted. You may find there are those in your group that can easily receive from others and those who resist being served.

Question 9. There are several ways that Elisha might be seen as going beyond the call of duty in his serving (though that's what serving is all about—going beyond the call of duty) the Shunammite woman. Note that Elisha could have given up on the idea of serving the Shunammite woman in the first place when he found she had no obvious need and was content. But as we have already looked at, he met her "felt" need by promising her a son.

Now in this time of crisis she runs to him for help. When Elisha sees her in the distance, he does not wait for her to get to them but sends his servant to her to ask if they are all right. He allowed her to grab hold of his feet when his servant objected. As soon as Elisha realized what the problem was, he instructed the servant to run to the child with his staff but ended up going himself because that was what the woman wanted.

Study 5. Love That Submits. 1 Samuel 3.

Purpose: To see how we can love one another by submitting to one another and to apply principles of submission to our lives.

Question 1. This question is just meant to get at the basics about Samuel and Eli. For instance, Samuel is young, under Eli's charge and sleeps in the temple. Eli was old and had sons who were rebellious and unrestrained by him. Just gather facts to become introduced to them. The question is not meant to delve into their attitudes, relationship with each other or with God. But as always, if the group answers some of the following questions when responding to this one, skip those questions when you get to them.

Question 6. Love is being actively concerned for another's best interest. Submission—not demanding our own way but bending our will to others—though difficult, is often love. It is putting the interest of others before our own. It is saying you are more important than my agenda or my getting my own way. It is taking on the attitude of Jesus who laid aside his agenda and power and became a servant.

Question 10. Listening to God is terribly difficult in this day of noise, rush and addiction to productivity. Amos wrote of the famine that the Sovereign Lord would send upon his people—the famine of "hearing the words of the Lord" (Amos 8:11). Joyce Huggett writes: "Many Christians, myself included, believe that prophecy has been fulfilled both in times past and in our own lifetime. For generations, the ability to listen to God's still, small voice has waned." She continues:

> But there are definite signs to suggest that, during the past two decades, the tide has been on the turn. Now it seems to be coming in, sweeping across our country with increasing force and bringing in its wake a renewed hunger to hear God's voice and an insatiable thirst for the stillness which is pregnant with God's presence. For this reason retreats are "in." Guest houses in monasteries and convents are full of people anxious to withdraw from the rush and tumble of twentieth-

century life, equally anxious to drop into the presence of God which they believe they might find in such a place. (Joyce Huggett, *The Joy of Listening to God* [Downers Grove, Ill.: InterVarsity Press, 1986], p. 11)

Note that it was in the quiet of the night that Samuel heard God's voice. Lead the group in discussing honestly where they are in listening to God, what their desires are concerning hearing his voice and what hinders them. There are many good books written with help in this area. Just a few of these are *The Joy of Listening to God* by Joyce Huggett, *The NIV Quiet Time Bible* (InterVarsity Press), *Celebration of Discipline* and *The Freedom of Simplicity* by Richard Foster (Harper & Row), and *Spiritual Disciplines for the Christian Life* by Donald S. Whitney (NavPress).

Study 6. Love That Prays. James 5:13-20.
Purpose: To grow in our love for others by praying for them faithfully.
General note. Don't be deceived. This is not a short study. Even though it covers only eight verses, you will need to gauge your time carefully. Several potentially controversial topics lurk in this passage—faith healing and the church's role in it is most notable among them. The place of prayer in one's life and thinking about love that prays also deserve time so the group members can get the concrete help needed in weak areas.
Question 3. I think we are encouraged to ask for help from the elders rather than it being imposed on us for several reasons. First, we will be more psychologically prepared to receive help when we have recognized our own need and asked for help. Second, this avoids forcing help on those who do not want it. Finally, this passage makes it clear that this is one option in dealing with illness. James does not say we have to call the elders.

Olive oil was used both internally and externally for medicinal purposes. It was also used in religious ceremonies of consecration (Ex 29:2) and purification (Lev 14:10-18). It symbolizes gladness, comfort and spiritual nourishment.
Question 4. This could be a time of giving exciting testimonies of God's great work in healing, or there may be those in your group who have been disappointed or hurt by God's response to their prayer for the healing of others.
Question 6. The promises in these verses seem clear and confident. Yet they may not be compatible with our experiences of praying for healing and not seeing the person recover. Often this situation is judged by others as our not having enough faith. That puts the emphasis on the person and their faith rather than on our God, who has made the promise. To try to simply explain God away or act as if we know his ways is sin. The first step in dealing with

this question personally and in leading the group is to humbly acknowledge, "I am not God, and I do not always understand God."

In the *New Bible Commentary* we find the following concerning this passage:

> The sick are to *call the elders of the church*. When a person is so ill that he or she cannot go to church, they want the people with the most faith in the church to come and pray. Normally, when the illness is not major, the rule is "pray for each other." The elders will act just like the disciples in Mk. 6:13 who must have learned it from Jesus, and anoint the sick person with oil as they pray, so their prayer is not only heard, but physically felt. The important fact is that the prayer is to the Lord and the anointing is done *in the name of the Lord.* It is the Lord, not the power of prayer or the oil, who will *raise him up.* And that is just how James promises that the Lord will respond to *the prayer offered in faith.* This is not a "hope so" or "maybe" prayer, but a prayer that shows secure confidence that God will heal because the elders have first listened to God and have received this confidence in their hearts. (p. 1367)

And from *The Epistle of James: Tests of a Living Faith:*

> That the gift of healing was possessed by the elders in each local church is difficult to assume. Nor is it probably correct to assume that James envisions that everyone who is thus anointed and prayed for will be miraculously healed. We agree that such prayer for the healing of the sick should properly be offered with the condition "if the Lord wills." But James' unconditional language seems best understood in accepting that "the prayer of faith" cannot be prayed at will but that it is given of God in certain cases, to serve His own loving purposes and in strict accordance with his sovereign will. Thus is it not just an ordinary prayer for another, however good and sincere it may be, but the prayer prompted by the spirit-wrought conviction that it is the Lord's will to heal the one being prayed for. Whenever God in his wisdom does not grant immediate healing, such a service has deep spiritual value for the believer in that it openly relates his illness to the will of God for him. ([Chicago, Ill.: Moody Press, 1979], p. 322)

Do not allow this topic to take over the study. Make your goal helping the group look more closely at who God is rather than having all the answers concerning healing prayer. If the discussion gets lengthy, invite the group to continue talking after the study and sensitively move on.

Question 9. See 1 Kings 17:1-7; 18:1, 42.

Question 10. The following two comments may help: "This phrase is used for serious departures from the faith (cf. Is. 9:16), not an occasional slip into sin. If it happens to a believer, someone should bring them back. . . . Rather than condemnation, restoration is the goal. And that is what James hopes will happen" (*New Bible Commentary,* pp. 137-38). Prayer is a privilege in all circumstances, notes Tasker, continuing, "The brother who has wandered away from the truth, forgetting the great doctrines of the Christian faith which he embraced at his conversion, and unmindful of those ideals of moral conduct based upon them, must always be a primary concern of the other members of the fellowship" (*The General Epistle of James* [Grand Rapids, Mich.: Eerdmans, 1979], pp. 142-43).

Study 7. Love That Comforts. 2 Corinthians 1:1-11.

Purpose: To consider how God shows his love to us through comfort, how Paul loved the Corinthians through his suffering and comforted them, and how we can express love that comforts.

Question 1. Often we quickly pass by the greetings in an epistle. This greeting is particularly important because of the topic of suffering and comfort. The first important fact is that Paul knew that it was God's will that he was an apostle. This means there was purpose in his ministry to the Corinthians and that what he suffered was under the jurisdiction of God—it was not accidental and not without meaning. Second, he is writing to "the church of God." It is as the church that we share in suffering and comfort and that we minister to each other. And finally, at no other time than in the midst of suffering is the grace and peace of God more important or the fact that he is our Father with his loving arms of comfort around us. Lead the group in digging into this wonderful greeting.

Question 2. It is easy to take God for granted. As you lead the group through this description of God, create an atmosphere of reverence and awe. This question is not asking "how *should* you respond?"; it's asking "what is really happening to you as you look at God through the lens of this passage?"

Question 4. Help the group to put themselves in Paul's shoes and to feel his suffering.

Question 6. Creating an environment of honesty and safety is one of your goals as the leader. You may have some in your group who feel God has not comforted or helped them. Accept these responses, listen carefully and reply gently. God can handle their questions. Don't feel like you have to come up with answers. Just being able to share pain is often a step in opening up to God.

Study 8. Love That Forgives. Matthew 18:21-35.

Purpose: To understand how much we have been forgiven and to grow in loving others by forgiving them.

Question 1. The seven times in Peter's question is symbolic, not literal, in meaning. Peter is asking, in effect, whether there should be any limit to his forgiveness. Note that Peter assumes that we are to forgive. He just wants to know how much. He probably felt his offer of seven times sounded very generous.

Question 2. Seek out answers that get to the root of human nature—selfishness, pride, self-righteousness and so on. Also be sensitive to responses about protecting ourselves from further hurt, being vulnerable when we forgive people and therefore let them back into our life. Forgiveness means experiencing the pain of the crime against you and choosing not to hold that against the offender. It does not mean denying that the crime ever took place. It does not mean not hurting. It does not even necessarily mean not remembering. Forgiving has to do with choices about your actions and responses.

Question 3. "Took pity" is perhaps more clearly translated in the KJV and NASB as "was moved with compassion" and "felt compassion."

Question 6. "Ten thousand talents combines the longest Greek numeral with the longest unit of currency. Even one talent was a small fortune; ten thousand was beyond the wildest dreams of ordinary people. A hundred denarii is not a negligible amount (a hundred days wages) but is a mere six-hundred-thousandth of the first sum" (*New Bible Commentary,* pp. 928-29).

Question 9. *The New Bible Commentary* says, "Thus in the light of God's incalculable grace to us, it is ludicrous as well as wicked for us to refuse to forgive others. The implied threat of v. 34 is made explicit in v. 35; God will not treat an unforgiving spirit lightly. This is the message of Matt. 6:14-15, and the parable reminds us of the way sins were described as 'debts' in the Lord's Prayer" (p. 929).

Question 11. Use this as a review question, looking back over the whole passage as you lead the group in thinking about how seriously Jesus takes forgiving.

Study 9. Love That Unites. Romans 12:1-21.

Purpose: To consider the practical aspects of presenting our bodies to God as spiritual worship and the harmony that develops in the body of Christ as we love one another.

Group discussion. If some group members do not appreciate music, adapt your question to what fits them: "How are you affected when you see beautiful harmony in nature, on a sports team, in art and so on?"

Question 1. Verse 1 refers to God's mercy: "It is only *in view of God's mercy* that his appeal becomes relevant and that our obedience of it is possible. As we recognize all (the word 'mercy' is plural in the Greek) that God has done for us in his Son, as Paul has surveyed in Romans 1-11, we realize that offering ourselves to God *as living sacrifices* is, indeed, a 'reasonable' act of worship" (*New Bible Commentary*, p. 1150). In verses 3 and 6 we see God's grace as the basis of what is said and done.

Question 2. Paul is encouraging us to look at our entire lives as acts of worship—our body and what it does, our mind and what it thinks—all lived out by his good and perfect will. We are an integrated whole—body, soul, mind and spirit. God wants and calls all of us.

Question 3. One summary of these verses is, accept one another where we are, as we are. We have different gifts and strengths and personalities, and all are part of the body. We need to allow and encourage each other to practice our gifts. Not uniformity, but diversity is the mark of God's work among us. We are given the warning by Paul to think of ourselves as we ought—in light of the special responsibility that God has given to us.

Question 5. This is an overview type of question. It will take you through the list in the passage. The following questions will ask more specifics about some of the things on the list. Again, if these questions are answered as the group goes through the list, that is fine. There is no need to repeat the question. Or if something on this list that is not covered in follow-up questions strikes you or someone in the group, it is great to pursue discussion of it.

Question 6. Philippians 2:3 says, "Do nothing out of selfish ambition or vain conceit, but in humility consider others better than yourselves." One definition of *love* is "to seek another's best good" or "to be actively concerned for another's best." Often this simply means putting another's needs before my own. It does not mean putting myself down, devaluing myself or not recognizing that I have needs. It does not mean doing for others what is healthy and best for them to do for themselves.

Phyllis J. Le Peau is an area director with InterVarsity Christian Fellowship in Chicago. Phyllis authored Woman of Rest *and the LifeGuide® Bible Studies* Acts *and* Love. *With her husband, Andy, she coauthored the LifeGuides* Ephesians *and* James. *Over 500,000 LifeGuides authored or coauthored by Phyllis Le Peau have been sold. She is also the author of three Fruit of the Spirit Guides (Zondervan). She is the mother of four adult children.*

What Should We Study Next?

A good place to continue your study of Scripture would be with a book study. Many groups begin with a Gospel such as *Mark* (20 studies by Jim Hoover) or *John* (26 studies by Douglas Connelly). These guides are divided into two parts so that if twenty or twenty-six weeks seems like too much to do at once, the group can feel free to do half and take a break with another topic. Later you might want to come back to it. You might prefer to try a shorter letter. *Philippians* (9 studies by Donald Baker), *Ephesians* (11 studies by Andrew T. and Phyllis J. Le Peau) and *1 & 2 Timothy and Titus* (11 studies by Pete Sommer) are good options. If you want to vary your reading with an Old Testament book, consider *Ecclesiastes* (12 studies by Bill and Teresa Syrios) for a challenging and exciting study.

There are a number of interesting topical LifeGuide studies as well. Here are some options for filling three or four quarters of a year:

Basic Discipleship
Christian Beliefs, 12 studies by Stephen D. Eyre
Christian Character, 12 studies by Andrea Sterk & Peter Scazzero
Christian Disciplines, 12 studies by Andrea Sterk & Peter Scazzero
Evangelism, 12 studies by Rebecca Pippert & Ruth Siemens

Building Community
Fruit of the Spirit, 9 studies by Hazel Offner
Spiritual Gifts, 12 studies by Charles & Anne Hummel
Christian Community, 10 studies by Rob Suggs

Character Studies
David, 12 studies by Jack Kuhatschek
New Testament Characters, 10 studies by Carolyn Nystrom
Old Testament Characters, 12 studies by Peter Scazzero
Women of the Old Testament, 12 studies by Gladys Hunt

The Trinity
Meeting God, 12 studies by J. I. Packer
Meeting Jesus, 13 studies by Leighton Ford
Meeting the Spirit, 10 studies by Douglas Connelly

OTHER BIBLE STUDIES BY PHYLLIS J. LE PEAU

Lifeguide® Bible Studies

Acts
Ephesians (with Andrew T. Le Peau)
James (with Andrew T. Le Peau)
Women of the New Testament

Woman of Character Bible Studies

A Woman of Rest

All Bible studies are from InterVarsity Press and are available at your local Christian bookstore. Visit our website at <www.ivpress.com> for more information.